AFTERWARDNESS

Mimi Khalvati was born in Tehran, Iran, and sent to boarding school on the Isle of Wight at the age of six. She has lived most of her life in London. She has published nine collections with Carcanet Press, including *The Meanest Flower*, shortlisted for the T.S. Eliot Prize 2007, *Child: New and Selected Poems 1991–2011*, a Poetry Book Society Special Commendation, and *The Weather Wheel*, a Poetry Book Society Recommendation and a book of the year in *The Independent*. Her pamphlet, *Earthshine* (Smith/Doorstop Books 2013), was a Poetry Book Society Pamphlet Choice and her *Very Selected Poems* appeared from Smith/Doorstop in 2017. She has held fellowships at the International Writing Program in Iowa, the American School in London and at the Royal Literary Fund, and her awards include a Cholmondeley Award from the Society of Authors and a major Arts Council Writer's Award. She is the founder of the Poetry School and a Fellow of the Royal Society of Literature and of The English Society.

AFTERWARDNESS

MIMI KHALVATI

CARCANET

First published in Great Britain in 2019 by
Carcanet
Alliance House, 30 Cross Street
Manchester M2 7AQ
www.carcanet.co.uk

A CIP catalogue record for this book is
available from the British Library.
ISBN 978 1 78410 799 4

Book design by Andrew Latimer
Printed in Great Britain by SRP Ltd, Exeter, Devon

The publisher acknowledges financial
assistance from Arts Council England.

for Marilyn Hacker

CONTENTS

QUESTIONS

You're smaller than you were or so you think.
You don't remember sinking quite so low
on other seats. Something has made you shrink
or else something has made the seatback grow.

You're a normal child, if a bit bewildered,
struggling to push the feelings down, the questions,
the stillborn questions never to be answered,
stretching to see a sky that simply darkens,

flying away from all you know with you
and someone sitting next to you, but who?
the only ones not gone or disappearing.

It's normal to feel trust. And you do, don't you?
Trust is a kind of seat belt, stretching, shrinking,
a *kammarband* you'll soon forget you're wearing.

TRANSLATION

I've heard them playing ball in Kacic Square,
children throwing languages in rotation –
their own, a new one, being made aware
as they leap, drop, pick up, catch, of translation,

the concept, long before they learn the word.
They learn translation is a kind of swap –
I'll give you *parandeh*, you give me bird.
But what if, whistling in some foreign treetop,

parandeh has long since flown out of mind
back to its own kind, never to return?
Then there are only local trees to fill

with bird, bird, bird; rows of them left behind
to chirp, chirp, chirp; sparrow, kittiwake, crossbill,
shrike and even bulbul to learn, learn, learn.

HANDWRITING

A line of c's is like a stylised sea
or seated monks obediently bowing;
cccc, line after line, spells safety,
sitting at a desk, doing joined-up writing.

This is the scaffolding – the alphabet
of posts and beams, the timber frame, the nave
of b's and d's whose pillars, if you let
the uprights slant, will topple on a wave –

the scaffolding and ark of spoken speech,
a chapel in which psalms and hymns become,
once you have learned to read the script, so clear.

There are wordings the ear alone can't reach,
strange idioms that make the mind go numb
but knowing how to write them helps you hear.

DICTATION

Like a bumblebee on a wild rampage,
stumbling against the sense that otherwise
ran as smooth as honey across my page,
one word I couldn't spell or recognise,

starting with k, or c, then double m
in the middle and holding in reserve
e r for the end, kept coming at random –
kommer? no, commer – till I lost my nerve.

Poor Deborah! Yoked to her father's muse.
And my poor daughter, darling. Who will be,
now she can't even see night stars, her hand,

her amanuensis? So let her use,
while she still can, her one good eye to see
wild bees, like commas, coming in to land.

ELOCUTION

She sat behind the door, squat as a toad
in a twinset and tweeds – my oracle.
How are the mighty fallen I intoned
as light poured in *in the midst of the battle!*

O Jonathan I moaned and through the pane
sun shone as though *O* were a sunburst window
flooding rays into my soul, *thou wast slain*
but who Jonathan was I wouldn't know –

I was Jonathan, the light and the sun
were Jonathan, my elocution mistress,
my first beloved, you were Jonathan

and *thy love to me was wonderful*, yes,
it was, it was, *passing the love of women,*
women and men. *How are the mighty fallen…*

BACKGROUND MUSIC

You may be in a café reading when,
after the intro, Billie Holliday
and *Easy Living* lure you out of Walden
and swing you in a trance out of the café.

You may be watching Shaun Evans as Morse
mostly to marvel at the mimicry
of his body language, so like John Thaw's,
when you're torn away, this time by Puccini,

away from the spires of Oxford to fall,
to fall as Tosca falls, defences fall,
that your heart breaks open a dungeon door

and griefs like prisoners crouched on the floor
bestir themselves and infant griefs like dolls
sleep through a bell that tolls and tolls and tolls.

BACKGROUND MUSIC (ii)

Music, being as wordless as they are –
these frozen griefs no trauma ever thawed,
these griefs that thought goodbye was au revoir
and thought the dead were living still abroad,

these unnamed griefs forgotten in a wasteland
where who and what and why have long dissolved –
seems, once brought to the fore, to understand
griefs neither time nor rhyme nor love resolved.

It's left to dreams of dull bewilderment
when wrong and right change places without cause
while witnesses, thank god, seem not to notice

to dredge up feelings of abandonment,
the day's debris for you alone to witness
a flood of shame that out of shame withdraws.

DREAMERS

Dreamers, before they lived a life of shadows,
a short life but long years of chasing fear,
before they found a room, sunblinds on windows,
an L-shaped desk, a home they know is here,

were children young as – most commonly – three,
with fringes, hairslides, hair too soft to hold them,
two hundred words in their vocabulary
and shapes of sentences in which to mould them:

sentence shapes like cradles for dolls to dream in,
like railway tracks and bridges, tunnels, sidings,
paradigms for journeys, returns and crossings,

first languages, half-formed, dropped at a border
Dreamers crossed and were too young to remember –
these students, immigrants, young men and women.

AFTERWARDNESS

An eleven-year-old boy from Aleppo
whose eyes hold only things no longer there
– a citadel, a moat, safe rooms of shadow,
'afterwardness' in his thousand yard stare –

years later, decades even, might turn around
to see, through the long tunnel of that gaze,
a yard, a pond and pine trees that surround,
as in a *chaharbagh*, four branching pathways.

Where do memories hide? the pine trees sing.
In language, of course, the four pathways reply.
What if the words be lost? the pine trees sigh.

Lost, the echo comes, lost like me in air.
Then sing, the pathways answer, sigh and sing
for the echo, for nothing, no one, nowhere.

To know your story is to understand
not only who you are and where you come from
– even if some imaginary homeland
is all you know, shall ever know of home –

but is also to understand the nature
of story, how to prime a palimpsest
for all successive stories, how to ensure
reference points gain valence from the first.

Hence, a love of narrative; and a mind
with an ingrained habit – established by
the underwriting of your own life story –

of near total recall it is unkind
to foist on one whose underscript is less
determined and who might feel envious.

CAFÉS

Envy them, the lonely, there by the glass,
there in the corner, staring into space
for as long as it takes the world to pass,
close up, far off, sprinkled like stars in cafés.

Envy them their orbit: how flagstones throw
a thin horned shadow of a bicycle
they take for Rocinante; how they borrow
longed-for landscapes, the islands of Lake Baikal,

a handful of lights from the Crimean plateau,
O envy them their raised sleeping-car window!
'Habituated to the Vast', how they move,

leaving a good tip, pulling on a glove,
paying with the exact change from their purse,
through spacetime in an abstract universe.

JOLANTA

I don't live here, according to Jolanta.
I only come here when she comes, she teases.
Between times, plants get watered, piles of paper
shrink or grow and a vase might spring sweetpeas.

But aside from a seismic shift on Wednesdays,
nothing's ever moved. Doors are door-stopped open.
Only the rooms float in and out of doorways,
plane trees in full leaf climb in from the garden

and plans to live elsewhere prove transitory.
Wagging a finger, 'See?' Jolanta scolds,
lycra-clad in citrus, her Marigolds

pumping a cloth black-grimed with nicotine
and tar from storage jars, 'You see, Mimi?'
So I do live here after all, you mean.

THE BRAG

I am known by sight in the neighbourhood
to shopkeepers, baristas, cab drivers.
There I go, there I come, in likelihood
alone, up and down the road, in all weathers.

I am on smiling terms with hosts of people.
There she blows with her silver hair, they grin,
staking out a beanrow, spouting the Bible.
Roadsweepers chat, guards greet me at the station.

Some call me lady, auntie, mammie – ask me
how I'm doing, endorse me with endearments,
watch my footing for me, rescue my bag.

Caregivers all! Small wonder if I brag
a little, graced with such acknowledgements
and such a large extended family.

Truth is, there's nobody she wants to find.
The very act of finding's frightening:
the human crouching in the bush, the blind
hump of hair and shoulder, the tell-tale clothing.

And being found's no better, backed to a wall,
shrinking on a dirt floor, hugging her knees.
But what if she were never found at all?
Left to herself with sacks of grain and chickpeas?

Once there would have been pickles, purées, lard,
mountains of melons, stores for every season,
a shop, a cookhouse, bathhouse, icehouse even

and, set on four sides of the inner courtyard,
one house for each branch of the family
no one beyond the high brick walls could see.

At its heart the pool, the blue rug of sky.
In the middle of my room, the kilim
with its fish and fowl. My propensity
for arranging furniture, it would seem,

in lines around the walls, leaving the floor
alone as the focal point, may be due
not to some dullness in the soul but more
to workings in the bloodstream, some residue

in subliminal memory of windows
that look forever inward, galaxies
that spin on carpets, geometric rows

of turquoise tiles ablaze with symmetries
inherent in physics; eyvans, porticos
of gardens brought indoors; a Sufi's verses.

In Cardiology, the corridor
is a bright blue stream of lino, a river
where, lined up like fishermen on a shore,
patients face patients ranged along the other.

One old fisherman, drumming on his cane,
sings softly to himself. A farawayness
surfaces like a shoal; a swirling chain
of choruses he strums like Orpheus.

Weddings, celebrations, birthdays, now quicken,
now subside, as his voice grows louder, quieter,
drifts down 'the narrows of the Arda River'.

Ali Kemal Ali! they call. Remember
Ali Kemal – that murdered politician
who was Boris Johnson's great-grandfather?

VILLAJOYOSA

So that a fisherman far out at sea
returning home as the sun sank or rose,
straining through fog, poor visibility,
could see, rowing toward Villajoyosa,

among seafront cottages on the shore,
his own abode and by it steer his course,
each house was painted a distinctive colour:
green, ochre, terracotta, sky blue, turquoise.

Of all the blossoms that are out in May,
the lilac – Persian lilac – shares the same
lodestar quality. Never to belong

back in the wild again but to a doorway
where a stranger might hear 'death's outlet song',
it holds the past, only the past in the doorframe.

The boy would always wear his coat indoors,
a long black cashmere, threadbare now and fraying.
He'd prop a folding magnifying mirror,
as though to shave before he started playing,

on top of the piano, tilt its face
towards his own, then bundled on the stool
still in his hat and coat, burning to trace
his double like Narcissus at the pool,

lean and stare in the glass, just stare, deaf-mute
to 'Don't you want to take your coat off darling?',
numb to the keyboard pressed against his knee.

Time made no sense to him. Minute by minute,
silent as time without him in it would be,
the boy, who was a man, sat fiercely staring.

DYSPHAGIA

We sat facing him, our backs to the window.
He sat facing the light which filled his eyes,
green as sea glass, with yet more light as though
to wash his skull of everything but skies.

We sat, disciples at the long ward table.
He wore a ribbed off-white garment that only
exposed how thin he was, near skeletal,
yet in demeanour upright, calm and friendly.

For days no food or drink had passed his lips.
We urged on him a phial of holy water
from Sarah's pilgrimage to Medjugorje.

Once, twice, he slowly blinked. He took one sip,
replaced the cap and thanked her. 'That's okay.
I'll leave it here,' she glanced around, 'for later.'

Everything that happens must happen here,
he thought, within the confines of the page.
Marshal your pencils then, master your fear.
Start with the sky, take the blue to the edge.

Leave no patch of white, no eye, no space.
Every block that is coloured in permits
relief and progress up the rooftop staircase,
flag by flag, to the wrought-iron parapets.

What is the void but love between two walls?
Don't fudge the corners where the angles dovetail.
Neither love nor fear can be drawn to scale.

Limbs that won't fit in if the trunk's too tall –
abbreviate. Let fortune be your draughtsman.
Look to your moon, black moon, your red half-curtain.

THE LESSER BRETHREN

Although she barely knew at school, at seven,
what a Moslem was or what Islam meant,
she proudly wrote: 'I know I'm not a Christian',
reassuring her mother, 'but for Lent

I have given up saying Honestly.'
And the truth was she liked going to chapel,
shuffling down the aisle, the passivity
of pews, her kneeler making her feel special.

Barred from a clear view of the altar rail
by rows of serge, blue laundered veils, she'd peer
instead at the fawn, vixen, rabbit, badger,

memorise the caption in bold serif,
see how His hands were drawn and wonder if
she really had a right to wear this veil.

TORBAY

It's not the headland pine above the scree,
the cliffs, two ships in fog, the scraps of light
between the lower branches that remind me
I could have reached them even at my height,

no, not the sight of sea that takes me back,
back to the Isle of Wight, a schoolgirl image
of standing under pines, flaking the bark,
rolling resin on my thumb, but the knowledge

that, wherever I stood, however steep
an incline and whatever blocked my view,
the sea was always there at walking distance,

as palpable in absence as in presence,
making roofs, trees, a hospital feel see-through
and those across the Solent just skin deep.

MARIA

Maria someone named her, painted her
block capitals Mediterranean blue
after they berthed her by a conifer
in grass to be the sweet spot in the view.

Not an oar in sight, her name freshly minted,
listing on the lawn so that rain and rust,
studded with pine needles from overhead,
pool on her starboard side, she lies in trust

to land now, England's apples, plums and pears.
Birds settle on her prow. I haven't seen them.
Nor can Maria see, just yards away,

where the Avon flows through the Vale of Evesham,
first canoes, kayaks, streaking past in pairs,
then green gloom like the sweet spot in a Monet.

Old stamping grounds are bruises to the heart.
Go visit them at dusk. Belisha beacons,
reflected in dark windows, flash and dart
like fireflies, synchronising light emissions.

Bollards at a junction, a spot for parking,
here is a nexus *entre chien et loup*.
A confluence of roads, a zebra crossing,
they synchronise the past and present too.

Bruising can effloresce like peonies,
slide down your body like a garter snake,
emerge in secret from a secret blow.

Still deeper in the tissues lies the ache
of underlying ruptures dusk alone is
discolouring in violet and yellow.

CHAMAELEONIDAE

Why did I say I minded things I didn't –
soul-making things I'd find too crude to name?
Or silently collude with heartfelt, well-meant
sympathy it seemed churlish to disclaim?

There is no childhood house that I remember,
no mother in it, merely surrogate
houses with mothers in them but no daughter,
where I would be their Alison or Kate.

In whose name can I talk of roots, of ruptures?
Melding with backgrounds, we fade into yours –
muted, cryptic, old world chameleons.

'Lions of the ground', we swivel horizons;
stalking the rainbow, we emblazon its colours.
These are our messages, these our emotions.

She wore the colours of these autumn trees,
carnelians, agates, grandiose and subtle.
She blended them in paintings, tapestries
of gardens, woods, perennially autumnal.

But when cataracts turned the tones too pale,
unknown to her, her flowers went fluorescent.
Then, when miniature work was bound to fail,
she took to painting liquid skies where pigment,

linseed oil, billowed of their own volition.
Skies hang silver-framed, windowed on my walls.
Live with a sunset, moon, a cloud formation

and soon they'll seem part of the furniture.
There's nothing new under the sun but palls
if we can't see its subtlety or grandeur.

MY MOTHER'S LIGHTER

From place to place, her lighter travels with me.
People admire it. Gold, faux tortoiseshell,
engraved with her initials, marked Colibri.
Vintage, cased; still not worth enough to sell.

Half-sentimental, half-dispassionate
and with no true attachment to or knowledge
of my own history, I try its weight
in my palm, run my thumb along an edge.

I flick the lid, the miniscule flint wheel,
and the same flame, its root invisible,
its calyx blue, bud gold, that she'd have seen

flares in the sunlight even as I feel
the wind hood heat up on my finger till
I snap it shut and rub my thumbprint clean.

Should you happen, crossing the upstairs landing,
to find the door ajar and dare to spy on
her sewing room, her instruments, her veining
tools and wire cutters, her gauffering iron,

you might be freaked by the dressmaker's dummy,
headless in the corner, its torso split
top to bottom as in an autopsy.
But should you happen to rush past and see it

out of the corner of your eye, her head
levitating just above it, head-height,
nearly joined to its neck, you'd die of fright.

For years I've kept that sketch stashed in my loft.
Instead, I picture roses cut and moulded
with tools you'd think too hard for silk so soft.

THE COURTYARD

Once we'd have jostled feral goats in here,
let them graze, scatter dung under our table,
suckle on fuschia buds, suddenly rear
by the fork of that dwarf Japanese maple,

then head off for the wild again; but now
there's just a robin flitting, spiderwebs
showing up in sun and the slatted shadow
a chairback casts, glowing before it ebbs.

Behind this courtyard other courtyards stand
the way parents, grandparents, lineages,
grand or humble, throng galleries in air.

May this backyard join their ranks anywhere
an arch we don't go through, on pilgrimages
we never take, harks back to Samarkand.

TWELVE

Twelve! Twelve! Twelve! Twelve! yells a despairing waiter.
But who is Twelve? Not the child by a river,
the Chinese child with an extra little finger
on each hand they call Shi'Er, who's four or five,

whose name means twelve, slipping out of a jungle,
out of a book, into a crowded café.
What *is* Twelve? Nominal? A numeral?
In her case, heartbreakingly both, I'd say.

Twelve. How quick the first consonantal cluster
to escape the teeth, how slow the dark *l*,
voiced *v*, to reverberate round the vowel,

an *e* that swells, that rhymes a temple bell.
Hedged by tall consonants, *e* in the centre
peals through a gap, an entrance for Shi'Er.

VERY

Very... the very first time that I heard
– or worked out what it meant since at that age
English was still a mystery – the word
'very', I thought it strange. A sudden passage

flashed through its scrollwork gate into the heart,
the very heart and all its imprecisions
hitherto silent, every distinct part
of language. Here, like steps, all the gradations

of feeling could be heightened, magnified,
for someone else to feel. Like guardian angels,
adjectives, adverbs, standing side by side

with lone words that might otherwise conceal
the very nature of their joys and troubles,
could qualify the world and make it real.

BUSH CRICKET

I picked out *What I Loved* by Siri Hustvedt
from that blue bookcase on a garden wall
under the fig tree. Having scarcely read
four pages, closing it, I see a small

bush cricket, her antennae waving, mask
What on the spine, aligning it exactly
with her lines. *What?* her body seems to ask,
threading it through a green transparency.

Now what? she asks a glass jar. Through the glass
she's slightly magnified as if through water.
She's upside down but thinks she's horizontal,

having hatched on the verticals of grass.
I think she likes diurnal roosting better
than asking questions so imponderable.

Never were texts less arid. Mrs Ramsay,
knitting, times her rows with the lawnmower,
seeds and thistledown float across Swann's Way
while grass keeps quoting 'glory in the flower'.

Insects fly on and off, streams mingle with
their sentences, wind muddles up their pages;
the sounds of carpentry, the coppersmith,
Lambrettas, punctuating passages.

And once a woman reading under trees,
bowed to her book, sitting oddly at ease
beside a statue of a woman also

bowed to her book, the one a perfect echo
of the other, summoned a double rainbow –
one arc in graphite, one in primaries.

POSTCARD FROM CRETE

I bought this one to keep. It half-recalls,
from years ago in Turkey, a verandah,
a flight of steps, flowers like waterfalls
on either side of scarlet, pink, magenta,

leading up to a tea-room in the middle
of nowhere where we once had Turkish breakfast.
The actual place seems immaterial.
What mattered were the chickens in the dust,

petrol cans potted with geraniums,
divans with rugs, an overhang of shade.
For people who like me belong nowhere,

places leave images we love to pair,
twin surfaces we've skimmed and overlaid,
cross-pollinating all our brightest vacuums.

THE STREET

So wide awake is spring now, eyes so open,
even the carpets long to fly outdoors
and lie, spread-eagled, carpeting the garden.
But is it only sun – bright visitors

from skylights, there at the top of the stairs,
braced to run down, brass stair rods at their heels;
is it only this sunless room which bears
a weight of shade so sculptural it feels

like Rachel Whiteread's *House* pumped full of concrete;
is it, not the sensation Jorie Graham
had 'how full void is', but of void itself,

only the membrane since it has no self,
the sweet tremble of void that makes the street
cast the prefatory glow of a poem?

It's civil twilight, sparkling over Euston.
On the pavement, a blind man's white stick whitens
and frosted footlights in the low walls turn
blind eyes too to the very paths they brighten.

Not as though there's anything there to see –
no homeless pile of sleeping bags and blankets,
no friendly drunks who want to be more friendly,
no smokers stubbing out last cigarettes.

In the blue hour, hobgoblin hour when fairies,
elves, 'quaint spirits' make mischief in a garden,
Friends garden, like an apron stage, stands empty.

At such an hour, Mary Shakespeare (née Arden),
under a sky still bright enough to read by,
enthralled her brood with gloaming, fireside stories.

The more she reads, the more her own life dims.
Stranded in the outrun, under a pole star
or in a land of paper gods, she skims
contours, heartlands that grow familiar,

akin more in their wild parabolas
to lives she always thought she could assume
given her youth, precocious as Lolita's,
than to this scanty plot, this narrow room.

Is it age that makes novelists now welcome
to implicate her in their machinations,
cast her as an addict, Arctic explorer

and throw her to the winds, fling her ashore,
then fetch her, like those missionary orphans
from Shanghai, staring out on deck, back home?

Blinded by sun, enter this quiet room.
Roses have entered it as quietly
and strawberries whose scent pervades the gloom
with danger signs of allergens a lady,

whose sneezes still erupt through lath and stucco,
can no longer bar servants bringing in.
Who was she? Where are we? In Melikhovo
with Uncle Vanya, Nina and Trigorin,

strolling in from the wooden porch, the garden,
summoned by a bell for the noonday meal?
Are we the guests? Whose fictions are we then?

And when we go, courteously as to leave
no living trace that we were ever real,
who will author proofs we ourselves believe?

LIFE WRITING

And if you do have a book with no plot,
story, timeline, no protagonists even
and no witnesses to events, it's not
so mind-numbing a proposition given

that there are some writers who want to write
about everything and are spoilt for choice
as to starting points and those who, despite
the conundrum that inviting a voice

out of a void would void the void of meaning,
nevertheless will listen out for nothing
and hearing it, think, as yesterday's wind

drifts pink almond blossom across their mind,
what's lighter than petals and yet, what heft
the tree bore, occluding the sky itself.

EGGS

From the first egg I ever drew, brown, speckled,
and pasted on a screen in kindergarden,
through all the eggs I ever ate, fried, scrambled,
boiled, poached, etc., down to this broken

yolk on a plate under my nose, my love
of eggs, in any shape or form, has grown.
Take the form: the prolate symmetry of
a spheroid, weightless when an egg is blown;

the air sac that expands with age and grades
an egg or backlights when you candle it
a blood red embryo; the sun-yolk shades

from marigolds the hens were fed at dawn;
the albumen: water out of which spirit
and embodiment, double-yoked, are drawn.

SEPTEMBER

Everything seems too beautiful to grasp.
I don't know what to feel, other than yearning
to stay forever neutral, on the cusp
of daydream, of a summer not quite turning,

its flotsam moving me to tears almost
and dapple on the streets, the dirtier
the better, always bringing home the contrast
of vague and real, of shadow-branch and litter.

'This vague and dream like world', Virginia says,
'without love, or heart, or passion, or sex'
might sound like a world we could live without

but 'is the world I really care about',
she pleads to Madge Vaughan in 1906,
and is the way I feel about today's.

Like skaters tracing figures on the ice,
figures of eight, circles that overlap
since no man steps in the same river twice,
on foot, by bus, we trace a mental map

of the places we pass so little changed
through all these years and of the men they link,
boyfriends, lovers, husbands, buried, estranged,
they conjure up like faces round a rink.

We are the widows, spinsters, divorcées
travelling round and round on loops and brackets,
scribbling on ice melting under our blades.

They are the phantoms, daemons, devotees
frequenting our haunts, the tutelary spirits
who, Plato wrote, conduct our souls to Hades.

IN PRAISE OF THE SESTET

If a kind of staring into your eyes,
your eyes without their glasses suddenly
meeting mine and making me realise
how nakedly you might have stared at me,

been staring all along behind thick lenses
(the sheet thrown back, the towel dropped and love
refused, withheld under your false pretences –
the sophistry, the sighs, the velvet glove),

'a kind of staring', Peter Sacks the scholar
opined 'into the eyes of the beloved',
were indeed the origin of the sonnet,

then God bless da Lentino who appended
a Sicilian folk song to such ardour
for us to dance, 'dance the undoing of it'.

Poetry startled me awake last night.
Stray lines, excited to be up so late,
streaked into view then melted out of sight
in light, without the lights on, grey as slate.

I listened, looked; half-blind, half-animal.
Cool air in a through-draught ruffled my fur.
I was a blind old tabby, dazed, forgetful,
letting the lines like mice race by the sofa.

Even in bed, Proust caught them by the tail,
batted them back and forth from clause to clause
till all the truth drained out of them and lay

pooled on the page. But my dim wits, my paws
were too illiterate to read their braille –
my mice would never see the light of day.

'PETITES SALISSURES'

is what Vuillard, working from memory,
called his small sketches and it intimates
the distortions, elisions and arbitrary
vanishing points that memory dictates.

And translations of *petites salissures* –
'little daubs' like the marks that dying moths
imprint with wings on dusty furniture,
'little bits of nothing' on tablecloths –

show how memory, reticent like mine,
fogged with the condensation of old age,
if squinting at a figure blurred in outline,

nameless were it not for her dress, will barely
disturb a woman steadying her passage,
reaching down an arm to a bentwood chair.

Down in an underworld that seemed to echo
my one abiding memory of chairs
placed in a ring but this time found in shadow
at the mouth of a crypt, down headlong stairs,

they came to visit me again in dream
or did I visit them? – close family
with no English but who would smile and beam,
laugh and chatter among themselves in Farsi.

What kind of monster was I and so loved?
The kind a married man with calf eyes woos
in some wild spot where all his girls have been?

Who listens to him croon, *Mara beboos,*
mara beboos – 'kiss me' – and is so moved
she falls in love, under the moon, at thirteen?

FACADES

What they both lack in beauty they make up for
in friendliness, incongruously adjacent,
the Aziziyeh Mosque sitting next door
to the Baptist Church in quiet contentment.

While the mosque gazes down on Kentish ragstone,
a slate pitched roof and gablet, neo-Gothic,
the church stares up at gold cupolas, fullblown
Ottoman tilework, columns of mosaic.

But what goes on behind facades God knows.
Witness returning exiles who might thrill,
after so long, to see their lineaments

etched on the faces of the crowd, yet still
feel all at sea and helpless to disclose
their new-found role as 'hidden immigrants'.

PHYSIOGNOMY

Not in the letters, diaries, memoirs, archives
his kin research, hoping to find the father
they never knew, absent throughout their lives,
do I find mine, but in his doppelganger,

twin stranger in the crowd – draped at the barber's,
in shirtsleeves, moccasins, playing backgammon,
caught on a newsreel among ayatollahs,
in Marks and Spencer waiting for his women.

Physiognomy's heady – lax cheeks, eyebrows
peaked like circumflexes, eyelids that sag,
traits that reach across the diaspora

of fathers to waylay an ageing daughter
checking herself in mirrors, smoked glass windows,
and smoke her out, looking like him in drag.

SMILES

These little smiles that fill my eyes with tears
mean nothing really, signals between women
who pass each other on the street as strangers,
as casual friends whose names are now forgotten

or local friends who stop to say hello
at bus stops, coughing little coughs like Lily,
Chinese Lily from Rouge, her shop, but also
English Lily who used to welcome me

by name and I'd respond in rhyme, whose sweet
manner seemed at odds with her black Goth gear.
She's gone to art school now and down the street

Bake Street café isn't the same without her.
Why tears though? I don't know – the loneliness
of women's lives, perhaps, that smiles express.

HOMA

She was an only child but like a sister.
Homa. The sort of person who could melt
your heart unless you hardened it against her.
'I've got a slug, a slug!' I'd yell and pelt

downhill, stuffing a dead leaf down her shirt.
Homa, so gullible, who never learned
how many hardened hearts there are to hurt
girls who love freely where love isn't earned.

How her eyes shone! She chattered like a bird.
She tapped out rhythms, tunes for me to guess,
used tomboy nicknames, however absurd.

Homa, so easily reduced to tears
by slights or sins she'd happily confess,
who mothered me through all my heartless years.

MY SIXTH BIRTHDAY PARTY

It was like a little wedding – the bride
in a cream crêpe dress that was miles too long,
her hair all wrong, the boy groom by her side.
But I knew why, why it had all gone wrong.

Where's Malijune? She's gone to *Suisse*, they said.
Suisse was a sword to brandish – *Aji maji*
la taraji! – and swing it round your head.
A steely blade, not a table knife, Daddy,

to cut the cake. *Suisse* was a pair of scissors,
a needle in her hand to hem my dress.
Suisse was my mother's glance, swift as a dart

to see it *did* look wrong, redo my parting,
slide a grip in and have me look like hers,
her child in *Suisse,* not here or somewhere else.

But what are all the court going to wear?
Seven sisters from Thailand, ranged in height,
each owning silk pyjamas, not one pair
but countless pairs, produced them on the night.

The Junior School, in Thai wild silk and pigtails,
filed in. The Emperor reclined. The little
kitchen-maid pointed and the nightingale
who, the Prime Minister surmised, might well

'have changed colour at the sight of so many
distinguished personages', singing hidden
in the wood, was a solo violin.

At all events, the evening was enchanting.
Death sat on the Emperor's heart but quickly
fled and the dead Emperor said 'Good morning'.

AZARINEJAD AND BEAR

Azarinejad put aside his turban
and his blue robe and squatted in the circle.
He turned to one child, then another: 'Children,
what did Bear want to do?' Was it a riddle?

One boy sat thinking, two boys picked their fingers.
One small girl smiled a big red smile while three
girls in hejab tried to smother their whispers.
They all knew the answer. They'd heard the story.

Azarinejad had opened the boot
of his old Peugeot, taken out the books
and read them *Bear Has a Story to Tell*.

So why not put their hands up? Why act mute?
Why be so bashful, sneaking little looks?
Wasn't Bear's story theirs to tell as well?

They came to see me off, bearing like Magi
gifts they unloaded from Chevys and taxis,
Korans in caskets, swords of gladioli,
pistachios rattling in cardboard boxes,

only to take them home again to rooms
where gladioli were returned to vases,
glass-fronted cabinets hid away heirlooms,
samovars endlessly refilled their glasses.

What if a heritage were lost en route?
In rosebud chintz, roomfuls of furniture
were stowed on board, down to a miniature

grand piano, also in Limoges porcelain,
painted with a Fragonard courting scene,
a maid and troubadour plucking his lute.

MEHRABAD AIRPORT (ii)

Sometimes you hear of someone dying when
you thought they'd died already years ago.
They come to life only to die again.
Bad memory can be so cruel although

close relatives who die abroad but live
well past their 100th birthday in the mind,
move about in their younger years, as active
or dependent, can prove it also kind.

So here they crowd in jet-black fifties hairdos,
pinstripes and polka dots, swing skirts and blouses,
siblings who rode and wore chadors on donkeys,

cousins who crouched diminutive in photos
deckle-edged like Pamuk's museum mementoes
in cabinets of curiosities.

VAPOUR TRAILS

Staring up at pure blue from down on earth,
we see them shining in the firmament,
the jets, the contrails, gliding back and forth
like deep sea fish, soundless and innocent.

Their exhaust particles and frozen vapours
show us, graphically, cause and effect:
in the silver bullet-nosed jets, the cause;
in trails like spinal x-rays, the effect.

It only takes a trigger, a single flight
in childhood, for example, early trauma,
to stretch the bare bones of the aftermath

into a lyric void beyond the finite
and knowable, a via negativa
cruising at altitude on plumes of breath.

'Dreamers': Undocumented migrants who arrived in the U.S. as children. Their name is taken from the DREAM Act – Development, Relief, and Education for Alien Minors – which has never been signed into law.

'Afterwardness': *chaharbagh* (Persian, meaning 'four gardens') is a quadripartite garden based on the four gardens of Paradise mentioned in the Qur'an.

'Scipto Inferior': the 'underwriting' or faint traces of former texts on a palimpsest.

'Cafés': the quoted phrase is from *Biographia Literaria*, S.T. Coleridge.

'The Introvert House': architectural term for a house built around an inner courtyard.

'Outpatients': 'The Narrows of the Arda River' (*Arda Boylari*) is a Balkan/Turkish folk song.

'Villajoyosa': the quoted phrase is from 'When Lilacs Last in the Dooryard Bloom'd', Walt Whitman.

'Dysphagia': difficulty in swallowing, which can be a side effect of antipsychotic medication.

'The Artist as a Child': after a sketch by Federico García Lorca.

'The Lesser Brethren': painting by Margaret Tarrant.

'Twelve': the poem draws on the novel, *In a Land of Paper Gods*, Rebecca Mackenzie.

'The Street': the quoted phrase is from 'The Mask Now', Jorie Graham.

'Friends House': the quoted phrase is from Shakespeare's *Midsummer Night's Dream*.

'The Older Reader': *The Outrun*, *Under a Pole Star* and *In a Land of Paper Gods* are novels by Amy Liptrot, Stef Penney and Rebecca Mackenzie respectively.

'In Praise of the Sestet': quotations are from *A Little Book on Form*, Robert Hass.

'One Summer Holiday': '*Mara beboos*' was an Iranian song popular in the 1960s.

'Facades': the term 'hidden immigrants' is taken from *Third Culture Kids*, David C. Pollock, Ruth E. Van Reken and Michael V. Pollock. I am indebted to the authors on whose themes I have drawn in some of these sonnets.

'My Sixth Birthday Party': *Aji maji la taraji* (Persian) roughly translates as 'abracadabra'.

'Junior School Production': the quoted phrase is from *The Nightingale*, Hans Christian Andersen.

'Azarinejad and Bear': the poem refers to *Bear Has a Story to Tell*, Philip C. Stead, and draws on an article captioned 'Iran's travelling cleric who reads to children' by Saeed Kamali Dehghan and a photograph in The Guardian, 29 August 2018.

'Mehrabad Airport (ii)': refers to Orhan Pamuk's The Museum of Innocence, after his eponymous novel.

ACKNOWLEDGEMENTS

Grateful thanks are due to the editors of the following publications in which some of these poems, or earlier versions of them, have appeared:

A Restricted View from Under the Hedge, *Acumen*, *Agenda*, *Ambit*, *Cimarron Review* (USA), *Exiled Ink e-mag*, *Long Poem Magazine*, *Peony* (Cam Rivers Publishing, 2019), *PN Review*, *POEM*, *Poetry and Audience*, *Poetry International*, *Poetry London*, *Poetry Salzburg Review*, *Quartet* (Avalanche Books, 2018), *Rusted Radishes* (Lebanon), *Smoke*, *Spring of the Muses* (Avalanche Books 2019), *Ten Poems about Childhood* (Candlestick Press, 2019), *The Compass*, *The Hippocrates Book of the Heart* (The Hippocrates Press, 2017), *The Mighty Stream* (Newcastle Centre for the Literary Arts/Bloodaxe Books, 2017), *The New Humanist*, *The North*, *The Rialto*, *Wasafiri*, *Wretched Strangers* (Boiler House Press, 2018).

My warmest thanks to Dr Nathalie Teitler and Dancing Words for producing the poem 'Afterwardness' as a poetry dance film with dancer/choreographer Ella Mesma and filmmaker Fiona Melville. https://bit.ly/2VR2rqE

I would like to thank Alfred Corn, Marilyn Hacker, Aamer Hussein, Christina Patterson, Myra Schneider and her workshop group, for their generosity in reading and responding to the manuscript or to individual poems and, in particular, Jane Duran for her thoughtful, painstaking comments and Michael Schmidt for his invaluable editing.